WordPress Websites Step-By-Step

The Complete Beginner's Guide
to Building a Website or Blog
With WordPress

By Caimin Jones

Praise for WordPress Step-by-Step

"Thank you! Thank you! Thank you! For an entire year I have searched for a book that would make it easy for me to understand WordPress. I am thankful for this step by step guide and I highly recommend it!"

LHAYWARD, Amazon.com reviewer

"It is an amazingly complete guide to creating and maintaining a WordPress site."

Lane P. Lester, Amazon.com reviewer

"I've been using WordPress for many years, and I learned an amazing amount about photos, formatting, plugins, and SEO that I didn't know before".

- B.L. Ochman, Internet marketer & social marketing consultant

Contents

About this book

Thank you for buying this book. My name is Caimin and I've been building websites for myself and clients since 1998. In 2008, I started using WordPress exclusively to make websites and haven't looked back. This guide is inspired by the problems I've seen people run into when starting out with WordPress.

But I'm not technical! Can you really show me how to make a website?

Absolutely.

This book is written for the complete beginner in plain English, leaving out long-winded technical explanations. If you can compose an email, I can show you how to use WordPress. Because this is a non-geek guide, it's been proofread many times to make sure it's the easiest guide possible. That said, if there's anything you're still not clear about, please feel free to email me and I'll try to help. My email address is on the last page of this book.

Don't forget to take a look at the additional free video tutorials that accompany this book. You'll find the link at the end of the book.

Why use WordPress?

By deciding to launch a website or blog using WordPress you've already taken a huge step in the right direction.

WordPress is a powerful, free publishing tool that's the single most popular way of publishing on the internet. It's used by Fortune 500 companies as well as millions of small and medium businesses, authors, photographers and bloggers to publish content, connect with visitors and make money.

It's also hands-down the easiest way to make a website or blog.

That might seem like a bold claim, but I've yet to see another publishing system that even non-technical people learn so quickly. As you'll see, you don't need to be a web designer or computer geek to build a great looking site.

That's not to say there isn't a learning curve - or there aren't things that will have you scratching your head when you first see them - but after reading this book, you'll have joined thousands of other readers who've used it to make a website they're proud of.

Once you get the hang of it, you'll find the standard WordPress features make building a website - including adding and editing content, image and videos - easy and fun.

When you're ready to get more adventurous, we'll look at how to personalize your web design and how to add complex features without knowing anything about web design or programming.

3 More Reasons to Use WordPress

1. Huge Number of "plugins"

Plugins are building blocks that let you customize and extend your site in powerful ways. With plugins you can create things like forums, membership sites or an online store - and a lot more besides. Many of these plugins are free. Imagine: You can build an online store in a few hours and it won't cost you anything but your time.

2. Search engines love WordPress

Just by making a few key tweaks - which I show you in the chapter on search engine optimization - you can structure your site for better rankings on Google, which means more visitors to your site.

3. Free, flexible web design "themes"

Themes are collections of templates that let you change your site design whenever you want without having to pay a designer or developer. As with plugins, there are free and paid options and we'll look at the advantages of both in the Themes chapter. But for now, rest assured that if you're on a budget and need to stick to free themes you can still create a professional looking website.

You'll learn how to use all these features in this book.

Once we've gone through the basics, we'll take a look at how to keep your site secure from hackers, how to set up automated backups and strategies for getting the first visitors to your site.

Because this is a practical guide, you'll get the most out of it if you read it while at your computer. Some things sound more complicated than they really are if you're not looking at the relevant screen.

Let's get started!

Part 1
Installing and Setting Up WordPress

WordPress.com vs. WordPress.org
- What's the Difference?

This first chapter deals with buying a domain, arranging web hosting and installing WordPress. If you already have WordPress set up and ready to go, skip ahead to the next section, Publishing Content With WordPress.

There are two versions of WordPress.

The version you'll find at WordPress.com is a hosted service. That means although there's nothing to install, you don't get as much freedom in the choice of web designs you use, you can't use your own domain name without an additional cost, and you can't add extra features to your site by using "plugins".

On the other hand, the version you'll find at WordPress.org is yours to download and use as you please. You can have your own domain name (which looks more professional), use any design and extend your site with as many "plugins" as you like.

This book is a guide to the WordPress.org version of WordPress. Don't worry if the idea of installing WordPress sounds off-putting - as we'll see in a later chapter, it can be done with a few clicks of the mouse.

How to Buy a Great Domain Name

A domain name is your personal address on the internet - like google.com is for Google and facebook.com is for Facebook. The price of a new domain name varies but a .com address shouldn't cost more than $15 a year. In fact, if you go to one of the big companies like GoDaddy you'll find them at around $9.

Choose a domain name carefully. Some common qualities of great domains are:

1. They're memorable

Short domains are usually easier to remember but they're often already taken. Instead, put two or three words together into a memorable phrase.

2. They're easy to spell

If you said your domain name over the phone, is there a chance someone would misspell it? The difference between RightNow.com and WriteNow.com is impossible to distinguish over the phone without spelling it out – and you'll soon get sick of saying, "That's write with a W...".

3. They avoid trademarks

Buying a domain that includes a registered trademark or the name of a famous company could get you into a lot of legal hot water, so it's best to avoid that problem by choosing an original name.

Other domain buying tips

Remember that it's perfectly acceptable to make up a word and use that. Famous examples of "nonsense" names include Flickr, Google and Yahoo. The same rules apply – make sure it's memorable and not easily misspelled.

If you're having trouble finding a name that's available, get creative by adding words like the, store, planet, etc. to the domain name. Some domain registrars like GoDaddy list free alternatives if your original choice is taken, which can help you think creatively.

Finding a domain for your name can be difficult - especially if you have a fairly common name. Try adding your profession or title to the domain. For example:

JaneDoeRomanceWriter.com
DoctorJohnDoe.com
LifeCoachJaneDoe.com

You get the idea. Sometimes you need to employ a little creativity to get a good domain name.

Once you've chosen a domain name I highly recommended buying it immediately. More than once I've spent hours finding a great, available domain name only to find the name had been taken by someone else when I tried to buy it later.

Which domain registrar?

There are literally hundreds of registration companies to choose from and you'll find the prices are near identical – the price of a couple of coffees. Personally, I've been very happy buying domains with GoDaddy.com.

How to Set Up Web Hosting

If you think of a domain name as being like the physical address of a store, then web hosting is the building the store is in. It's the central place where everything to do with your website - content, images, etc. - is stored.

Although there are thousands of web hosting companies to choose from, my advice is to stick with one of the well-known companies like Bluehost, Dreamhost, HostGator or MediaTemple.

These are big name hosting companies that offer reliable services at a good price.

Because all the big providers have a similar set of features - including a control panel for setting up email addresses, and checking site statistics etc. - the major deciding factor between the companies is price.

Some of the best deals around are the Hatchling and Baby plans from HostGator.

With either plan you get:

- Unlimited disk space, bandwidth and email usage
- 99.9% Uptime Guarantee
- A 45-day money back guarantee

The only difference between the Hatchling and Baby plan is the number of websites allowed. The Baby plan allows you to have unlimited domains, Hatchling only one.

You'll find HostGator at http://www.hostgator.com - I have a coupon code I created for friends and clients that'll give you 25% off. Just use *genius25off* at the checkout.

Whichever hosting company you choose, they all have a one-click installation process for WordPress, which saves you having to install it yourself. In the next chapter we'll run through how to set up WordPress on each of the hosting companies above.

Installing WordPress the Easy Way

The easiest way to install WordPress is to use the one-click, automatic installation process that all good web hosting companies provide.

Different web hosts have different names for this feature, but it's the same idea - you fill in a simple form and all the tricky technical stuff like uploading files and setting up databases is done for you.

Below are quick guides on how to set up WordPress on the most popular hosting companies:

Bluehost
Inside cPanel, choose *Software/Services* and then click *Simple Scripts*. On the next page choose WordPress and click the *Install Now* button. Next, choose the website you want to use with WordPress, give your site a title and choose a username and password. Click the *Complete* button to install.

Dreamhost
In your control panel, go to the *One Click Installs* page under *Goodies*. Click the *Advanced* option and then select WordPress as the program to be installed. Select the website you want to use WordPress on from the dropdown menu at the bottom of the page. Click the *Install* button.

HostGator
From your *cPanel*, choose the *Software/Services* section and then click *QuickInstall*. Under *Blog Software*, click WordPress, then *Continue*. If needed, change the *Application URL* (this is where WordPress will be installed). Choose a blog title and fill in your email address. Click *Install Now*.

Media Temple
In your Account Center, click the *Admin* button to access the Control Panel. Select *1-Click Applications* from the options. Choose *Add a New Application*. Click the *Start* button next to WordPress. On the next page, type the domain name you want to use with WordPress - there's no need to change the other settings if you don't want to. Click *Install*.

Installing WordPress on other hosts

Most good web hosting companies have a simple installation process that's very similar to those above. If you can't find it, contact the support team.

Manually installing WordPress

This isn't difficult but you do need to be comfortable using an FTP program to upload files to a web server. If that sounds like you, WordPress provides an excellent step-by-step tutorial:

http://codex.wordpress.org/Installing_WordPress

Unless you have a good reason to install manually, it's much easier and quicker to use a one-click install option.

Logging In and Out of WordPress Admin

Websites made with WordPress have two sides to them. There's a public site that every visitor can see and a password-protected admin area where you login to edit the site content and make other changes.

To login to your admin area, go to this link in your browser:

http://www.*yoursite.com*/wp-login.php

Don't forget to change *yoursite.com* to your own domain. Once there, type in your username and password and click the login button.

Tip: If the web address above doesn't work, it means the WordPress admin area is installed in a separate folder on the web server. To find out the correct login address go to your control panel or ask the support team at your hosting company to tell you the correct address.

Once logged in, you'll see the WordPress Dashboard. The important part of the screen is the vertical navigation menu on the left. You'll see it has headings like *Posts*, *Media*, *Pages*, and so on.

This is the main menu and you'll see it on every page of the admin area.

In this book, an instruction like "Go to *Posts > Add New*" means, "On the left menu in WordPress Admin, click on *Add New* under *Posts*.

How to log out of WordPress

If you use a shared or public computer it's a good idea to log out each time you've finished using WordPress. You can log out from any page by rolling your mouse over your username at the top right of the page and clicking *Log Out*.

5 Settings to Customize Before Launching Your Website

There are a five settings you should change before starting. Most of these settings you'll find on the same page under *Settings > General*.

1.Tagline

You'll find this near the top of the page, under *Site Title*.

When first installed, WordPress fills this with the words, "Just another WordPress blog". That's not very helpful to visitors, so change the tagline to something that better describes your website.

Use a sentence that says concisely what your site is about and would make a user want to click your link if they saw the description in search engine results.

For example, if your site is about Italian food you could use a tagline like, "Discover the secret tips and tricks for creating authentic Italian cooking in your own home".

2. Timezone

This setting makes sure the times and dates you see in WordPress are correct for your timezone.

If the timezone is incorrect, just change the select box to your timezone.

3. Time and Date Formats

Under the timezone selector, you'll see *Time Format, Date Format* and *Week Starts On*. These affect the way the time and date is displayed on your site, so change them if you don't like the default settings. There's no need to change any of the other settings on the page at this point. Don't forget to click *Save Changes* before you leave the page.

4. Change Your Permalink Settings

Permalink is a fancy, tech name for a web address. By default, WordPress makes permalinks that follow this format: *http://www.yoursite.com/?p=123.*

Unfortunately, the *?p=123* part isn't a format search engines like very much. They usually rank sites higher if they use real words in their permalinks instead of numbers and weird characters.

That means a web page with a permalink like *http://www.yoursite.com/?p=123* usually appears lower in Google search results than a page that has a permalink like *http://www.yoursite.com/your-post-title/.*

Because of that, it's a good idea to change your permalink settings before you start publishing content. Go to *Settings > Permalinks*. Select *Post name* under *Common Settings* and click *Save Changes*.

That's all there is to it. You only need to make this change once. Now, if you write a post with the title "Productivity Tips", WordPress will create a search engine friendly, professional looking permalink of:

http://www.yoursite.com/productivity-tips/

5. Delete the sample content

When you first install WordPress, it comes with a sample page and a sample post. Because these two pages don't contain anything useful, it's best if you delete them so they don't get confused with your own content.

To delete the sample blog post called "Hello, World!", go to *Posts > All Posts*. Run your mouse over the "Hello, World!" title and you'll see a few links appear under it. Click the *Trash* link to delete the post.

To delete the sample page called "Sample Page", you do something very similar. Go to *Pages* > *All Pages*.

If you mouse-over the title you'll be able to see and click the same *Trash* link.

That's it, now let's start adding <u>your</u> content.

Part 2
Publishing Content With WordPress

How To Write and Publish a Blog Post

This section deals with the core features of WordPress. You'll learn everything you need to know to get your first pages online, including:

- How to write and publish blog posts
- Adding images and videos to your posts
- Using categories and tags to help users navigate your site
- How to allow and moderate comments

We'll concentrate only on what you need to know to publish your first blog posts and pages. In later chapters we'll get to the more advanced things you can do with WordPress.

To add a new post, go to *Posts > Add New*. You'll see a screen that looks like this.

This is the *Add New Post* screen. You'll see this same screen whether you're writing a new post or editing an old one. The only difference is the name - if you're starting a new post this page is called *Add New Post*, if you're editing an existing post this page is called *Edit Post*.

There's quite a lot on this page, but we're going to concentrate on the two text boxes in the middle area of the page.

The top box is for the title of your post. Go ahead and add a title - anything will do because we're just testing at the moment.

The really large box underneath is where the rest of your post content will go. When you come to add text, images or videos, it all goes in this larger box.

To add text, just click inside and start typing.

Now you've got some sample text, let's look at how to format it. All the formatting tools are found on the toolbar that runs along the top of the post box.

Note: Above the toolbar icon, there's a button that says *Add Media*. That's for adding images and videos to posts, which we cover in the next chapter.

Formatting text - adding bold, italics, links and more

Let's start by making some of the text bold. First, highlight the text you want to become bold in the main text box. Then click the first icon (**B**).

That's it. It's the same idea for most of the other formatting buttons. To put text in *italics*, highlight the text you want to format and click the *I* button. For a strikethrough effects, click the ~~ABC~~ icon which is third from the left.

You can see that formatting text in WordPress is pretty similar to using Microsoft Word, LibreOffice or another word-processing program.

Underlining and changing the font color

The two buttons for these format styles are on the second row of the toolbar which is hidden by default. If you can't see two rows of icons, click the icon on the far right that looks a little like a keyboard.

This will open the second toolbar. Below you can see the toolbar fully open, with the **U** and **A** icons used for underlining and changing the font color on the lower toolbar.

Removing formatting

Highlight the formatted text, then click the icon halfway along the lower toolbar that looks like an eraser.

Let's go through what the other buttons - some are more obvious than others.

Creating bullet points

Starting with the top toolbar, the fourth and fifth icons are for creating bullet point lists - either with or without numbers. Just highlight the text you want to become a bulleted list and click the list icon.

Adding quotes

Next, the icon on the top bar that looks like a quote mark. This indents the text and is used on many websites to indicate a quote or excerpt from another source.

Aligning text

In the middle of the top toolbar are three icons for making text left, center or right justified. Most of the time you'll probably want to stick with the default left justification because it's easiest to read.

Adding web links

Next to those three icons are two that are usually dimmed and inactive. These are for adding and removing links to other sites, or to other pages of your own site.

To add a link, highlight the word or phrase you want to become the link. Once you've highlighted some text, the two linking icons will become active. Clicking the one that looks like a chain link will bring up the *Insert/edit link* box.

What you do next depends on what you're linking to.

Linking to a page on another website

Type or paste the link into the *URL* box and click the *Add Link* button.

Linking to another page or post on your own website

Click the heading towards the bottom of the box that says *Or link to existing content*. A panel will open showing the most recently added content. If you haven't yet added any pages or posts you won't see anything listed.

Click on the title of the post or page you want to link to and then *Add Link*.

Editing or removing links

To remove a link, click on the word or phrase that's linked and then click the broken chain link icon. If you want to edit a link - maybe to make it point to a different page - click the linked text in the editor and then click the chain link icon. This will bring up the *Insert/edit link* box again so you can make changes.

The More button

The icon next to the link / unlink button inserts something called a *More* tag. This allows you to set the point where the "Continue reading" link appears for that post when it's listed on the homepage.

For example, if the More tag is used like this in the editor...

...it will look like this on the homepage:

Do you want to know a secret?

Continue reading →

Distraction Free Editor

To the right of the spell-checker, there's an icon that has a box with arrows pointing to the corners. This switches the post editor to the *Distraction Free Writing* mode. In this view, almost all of the other buttons and boxes on the page are hidden, leaving a minimalist interface with fewer distractions.

Many bloggers love this feature because it helps focus the mind on writing blog posts and gives you more room to do it.

You can switch back from *Distraction Free Writing* mode to the regular editing screen any time by clicking the link at the top left of the page that says *Exit Fullscreen*.

Adding headings

On the left of the lower toolbar in the normal editor is a dropdown menu for a number of preset formatting styles. You'll find several heading sizes from large to small, as well as a couple of other preset styles. To apply a heading or style, highlight the text you want to format and select a style from the dropdown menu.

Tip: When you're writing a blog post, don't go too crazy with text formatting. Occasional use of bold, bullet points and headings are a good idea because they make posts easier to read, but too much formatting is distracting and looks unprofessional.

Inserting special characters like © or ®

Click the icon with the **Ω** symbol on the lower toolbar. Choose the character you want from the *Select custom character* box that appears.

Copying and pasting text from Microsoft Word

Even with all the formatting tools in WordPress, some people prefer to do the main part of their writing in Microsoft Word. It's just what they're comfortable with.

The trouble is, Word uses lots of complex formatting that's not suited for use in a web page. That means if you paste directly from Word to WordPress you'll probably have problems with strange formatting and weird characters.

But there is a safe way to copy and paste from Word:

1. Copy your text as normal from Word.
2. Place your cursor where you want the text to be in the WordPress editor.
3. Click the icon with the **W** on it in the middle of the lower toolbar.
4. Paste your Word text into the box that appears and click *Insert*.

This simple extra step converts the text into a usable format for the web while keeping the bold, italics and other styling intact.

Previewing, saving and publishing

When you've finished working on it, you need to do one of three things with your post:

Preview
See exactly how the post will look when viewed by visitors.

Save Draft
Save all the work you've done, without publishing.

Publish

Save and then Publish the post on your site.

The controls for all three options are in the same place - at the top of the right under *Publish*.

Previewing your post is easy - just click the *Preview* button. A new browser tab will open showing your post as it will appear on your website. If you see something you want to change, close that browser tab, go back to the Edit Post screen to make your changes, then click *Preview* again.

You can do this as many times as you like until you're happy with the post. Nothing will appear on your site until you actually hit the *Publish* button.

To save your post and continue working on it later, click *Save Draft*. This saves without publishing.

Ready to publish your post? Just click *Publish*.

How to schedule a post for future publication

There's one other publishing option you should know about - scheduling a post.

Sometimes you may have finished a post but don't want to publish it immediately. Let's say you write a post on Monday about a special offer that will be available on Friday. With post scheduling, you can tell WordPress to publish your post automatically on Friday.

Just above the blue *Publish* button you'll find text that says *Publish immediately*. Clicking the *Edit* link next that allows you to change the publishing date and time of the post.

After you've adjusted the date, click OK. The *Publish* button will now say *Schedule* instead. Click the *Schedule* button and you're done.

Editing posts later

Going to *Posts* > *All Posts* will show a page listing all the posts you've created whether published, drafts or scheduled.

Clicking on the title of the post you want to edit opens up the post in the *Edit Post* screen, which is the same screen we've been using in this chapter. The only difference - except for the title - is that if you're working on a post that's already published the *Publish* button is called *Update*.

Revisions

WordPress automatically stores previous versions of your posts and pages, so that you can revert back to a previous version easily.

Click open the *Revisions* panel on the edit post / page screen (if you don't see the Revisions panel, click Screen Options at the top right of the page and make sure Revisions is checked).

Clicking the date of a previous version lets you compare it to the version of the post currently being used. You'll see the two versions side by side with the differences between the two highlighted.

To use the older version, click the *Restore This Version* button.

You can compare other versions of the post buy clicking the *Next* and *Previous* buttons. To keep using the current version of the post - without restoring a previous version - hit the browser back button or click the post title at the top of the page.

Autosaves

To help protect your work if you forget to save it, WordPress also makes a backup every 60 seconds. You'll see these versions listed as *Autosave* in the list of revisions.

There is only one autosave version of a post or page at any one time.

WordPress also saves a backup copy within your browser if you lose your internet connection before you get chance to click Update / Publish. If that happens you'll see a prompt at the top of the screen letting you know how to restore the autosave version.

What about the other features?

You probably noticed several features - like categories and tags - that we haven't mentioned yet. That's because I wanted you to be able to publish a basic post right away, without worrying about these more advanced features.

Categories and Tags we'll look at in a later chapter. Next, we'll go through how to add images to your posts.

Adding Images & Image Galleries

Pairing a well-written blog post with an eye-catching image is a great way to help your posts get shared more on social networks, so it's worth spending a little extra time to find a good image.

Although you can just do a Google search for an image, there are two problems with that.

First, the results are sometimes pretty sketchy. The images are often unprofessional and don't offer much variety. Second, images are usually subject to copyright and shouldn't be used without payment.

Luckily, there are several resources for good quality images that are free. The only "payment" that may be required is a link back to the photographer's website. You should always check to see if that's a condition of use.

Here are a few of my favorite places to find free images:

http://www.flickr.com/creativecommons/
http://photopin.com
http://www.wikipedia.org
http://www.iconfinder.com

How to add an image to a post

On the *Edit Post* or *Add New Post* screen put your cursor where you want the image to be shown in your post. Then click the button above the formating toolbar that says *Add Media*. The *Insert Media* pop-up panel will appear.

If you've already uploaded images, the *Insert Media* panel will show the *Media Library* - a collection of all the images you've previously used in WordPress. Having a handy library like this makes it easy to re-use an image from a previous post without having to upload it twice.

If you haven't yet uploaded any images, your *Media Library* will look like the screenshot above and show "No items found" instead of an image collection.

Uploading an image

There are two ways to add an image. You can either use the *Select Files* button to use an image on your computer, or you can simply drag and drop the image you want to use into the pop-up panel. Whichever method you choose, after a second or two your image will appear at the top of the panel.

When the image is selected (as in the screenshot above), a panel appears on the right called *Attachment Details*. In this panel you can do two things - add captions to the image and control exactly how it will appear within the text of your post.

Let's take a look at each.

Setting Attachment Details

First let's add captions and a description. You don't have to do this but it's a good habit to get into because it makes it easier to find images in the library and captioned images make sites look more professional.

For speed, I usually type the same short title for *Title*, *Caption* and *Alt Text*. The *Title* is used inside the *Media Library*, *Caption* is displayed under the image on your website, and *Alt Text* is used when the image can't be displayed - in the screen-reader of a visually-impaired visitor, for example.

The *Alt Text* is also used by search engines to understand what an image shows and is helpful for search engine rankings. We'll cover this more in the later chapter on search engine optimization. For now all you need to know is that it's a good idea to fill in the *Alt Text* field with a short, meaningful description.

The *Description* is a longer summary of what the image is about, which gets displayed on the *Attachment Page* (see below).

Editing Attachment Display Settings

These three settings control how the image looks within the text of your blog post.

The first, *Alignment*, sets whether the picture will flow to the *Left*, *Center* or *Right* of the text around it. Leaving the *Alignment* setting at the default *None* will leave the image with a space to the left - the text won't wrap around the image at all. The image below shows you how each type of image alignment looks.

On the left is *None*, followed by *Left*, *Center*, and *Right* alignment.

The next setting in the *Attachment Panel - Link To -* determines where the user will be taken if they click on the image.

The choices are:

Custom URL

This can be any web address. You might use this if you're showing a picture of a product from Amazon and you want people clicking the image to be taken to the Amazon product page.

Attachment Page

This is preset by WordPress and leads to a page that contains the full-sized version of the image. If you added a *Description* to the image it will appear on this page.

Media File

Similar to *Attachment Page*, except the user will see the full file without a page surrounding it.

None

With this option, no link is added so nothing happens if the image is clicked.

Finally, you need to set the size of the image.

As well as the original version, WordPress automatically generates two other sizes - Thumbnail and Medium. Unless your original image is small to begin with, it's likely you'll want to use one of these smaller sizes in your post. Large pictures can make posts difficult to read because the image pushes the text to the far side of the browser.

Once you've set all the options, click the blue *Insert into post* button. You should now see the image inside the post editing box.

Editing an image

If you decide to make the image larger or smaller, change the alignment, or edit the caption or other text, click on the image and then click the edit icon that appears at the top left of the image.

An image editing panel appears that allows you to fine-tune your image.

Make your changes then click *Update*.

Deleting an image

If you decide not to use an image you can delete it by clicking the delete icon that appears towards the top left of the image when you click it with your mouse.

That will remove the image from your post but it doesn't delete it from WordPress. If you change your mind - or want to use the image in another post - you'll still find it in the *Media Library*. Just click the *Add Media* button again to see it.

If you want to delete an image completely from WordPress - including the library - click on the image within *Media Library* and then click *Delete Permanently* under *Attachment Details* on the right.

Creating an Image Gallery

An image gallery is like a virtual photo album and it's a great way to share lots of images with your visitors within one page. You'll have seen galleries in action before on sites like Facebook and Google+.

WordPress includes a quick and easy way of putting together an image gallery. It will generate thumbnail images automatically and arrange them in a grid with links leading through to full-size images.

The first step is to upload all the images you want to include in your gallery. Use the same process as above - but don't click the *Insert Into Post* button after uploading each image. If you want to make an image gallery from images that are already in the *Media Library* there's no need to upload them again. Just click the *Add Media* button to bring up the *Insert Media* screen.

From the left column of the *Insert Media* screen, click on *Create Gallery*.

Now click to select each image you want to use in your gallery. Don't worry about the order - you can change that later. Clicking on an image once adds it to the selection, clicking it again removes it from the selection.

Once all the images you want to use are selected, click the *Create a new gallery* button to the bottom right of the screen.

Now you'll find yourself on the *Edit Gallery* screen. Here you can drag and drop the images to change the order as well as add or edit image captions.

Under *Gallery Settings* you can also decide how many columns to use for your thumbnail pages. WordPress uses three as a default and that looks good with most design themes, so usually you won't need to change it. When you're done, click *Insert gallery*.

Like a single image, you can edit or delete the gallery by clicking it and then selecting either the edit or delete icon.

Adding Videos

There are two ways to add videos to your WordPress blog - uploading to the *Media Library* or playing them via YouTube or another video hosting site (called embedding).

The YouTube / embedding method is by far the easiest.

There are only two steps.

1. Go to the YouTube page for the video you want to show on your blog.
2. Copy and paste the URL into the post editing box in WordPress.

That's it. You don't need to use the Add Media button or to do anything with the link - just copy and paste it in as is.

Click the *Preview* button and you'll see WordPress has done all the hard work of creating a YouTube video player and embedding the programming code to make it work in your post.

This nifty feature is called *oEmbed* and it works with more that just YouTube videos. You can use the same trick to show videos and content from many of these sites too. Here's the complete list:

blip.tv
DailyMotion
Flickr (both images and videos)
FunnyOrDie.com
Hulu
Instagram
Qik
Photobucket
PollDaddy
Rdio
Revision3
Scribd
SlideShare
SmugMug
SoundCloud
Spotify

Twitter
Viddler
Vimeo
WordPress.tv (a site featuring WordPress video tutorials)
YouTube

Uploading a video to the Media Library

Aside from being more complicated, you may also run into file size limits with longer videos. This method also doesn't create a user-friendly video player like the YouTube method does.

Instead, it just creates a link that opens the video in a new browser tab. There are ways to beautify the way this process works, but for that we need an add-on feature called a Plugin, which we'll cover later in the book.

If I haven't put you off, here's the manual way of adding videos:

Place your cursor where you want the video link to appear in your post, then click the *Add Media* button.

The *Insert Media* panel will appear. Click the *Upload Files* link towards the top and then - just as with images - either select a video from your computer or drag and drop it into the library.

After your video is uploaded, you'll see the *Attachment Details* panel on the right. This works the same way as it does for images. Once you've made any changes you want to, click *Insert into post*.

Adding Audio

Without using a plugin, adding audio to WordPress is a very basic affair.

Your only choice is to upload the audio file using the *Add Media* button and follow exactly the same steps as for adding images and videos.

When you click *Insert into post* WordPress will add a link that will open the file in the audio player on the user's computer.

As with videos, there are more sophisticated ways of playing audio on a WordPress website but for those you'll need to use plugins, which we cover in a later chapter.

That said, some audio sites are supported by the *oEmbed* feature mentioned in the previous chapter. These include *Rdio*, *SoundCloud* and *Spotify*.

Keeping Organized: Categories and Tags

Categories and Tags are two similar but slightly different ways to organize posts and make it easier for visitors to navigate your site.

Categories

Categories collect together sub-themes of the main topic. As well as helping to make a subject more manageable, they also make it easy for visitors to find blog posts on a similar theme. Anyone visiting a site about European cooking, for example, would immediately understand that categories called Italy or France contain posts on cooking from those countries.

Categories are flexible. You can create as many as you need and even make subcategories within other categories.

Creating, editing and deleting categories

There are two places in WordPress where you can add categories, but only one where you can also edit and delete them.

You can create new categories directly on the *Add New Post* or *Edit Post* screen. At the bottom of the *Categories* panel on the right is an *Add New Category* link. Clicking that pops open a text box. Type in a name for the new category and click the *Add New Category* button.

The new category will be created and you'll see it's selected, meaning the current post will be placed in that category when you publish or update the post.

You can't edit or delete categories from this screen. To do that, you need to go to *Posts > Categories*. On the right you'll see a list of all your categories. If you haven't yet created any categories you'll see only one category called *Uncategorized*.

On the left is a more advanced version of the *Add New Category* form. Although there are extra fields, you can safely ignore those and just fill in the *Name* - and choose a parent category if you're adding a subcategory to an existing category - and let WordPress take care of everything else automatically.

Running your mouse over the category titles on the right side of the page brings up a sub-menu of options. It's from here you can delete a category or edit it.

Tip: Deleting a category doesn't delete the posts in the category. Instead, they'll be reassigned to the default category set under *Settings > Writing*. If you want to delete all the posts in a category, go to *Posts > All Posts* and use the filter dropdown in the middle of the page to show only the posts from that category. Then use the *Bulk Actions* menu towards the top left to delete all the posts in one go.

Tags

Tags are like terms in a book index. They help you find precise information that might be spread across multiple posts. In our cooking site example, a post about creating the ideal Spaghetti Bolognese sauce would be in the Italy category but could also have tags like pasta, spaghetti, meat dishes, and so on.

The difference between categories and tags is a subtle one and not worth sweating about. While tags were frequently used a few years ago, fewer and fewer sites use them now.

In fact, unless you have a compelling reason to use tags, there's no reason to.

So what's the best way of organizing content?

Here's a simple plan that works well for 90% of websites. Create five or six (maybe more) categories that cover the main areas of your subject.

Put each blog post in the single most appropriate category. Leave it at that. Your site will be simple, well-organized and easy to use, which is exactly the kind of site visitors and search engines love.

Allowing Comments & Dealing With Spam

As well as being an easy way for visitors to leave feedback, comments help you discover more about your audience and the posts they enjoy reading the most.

Taking the time to respond to each comment is also a simple but effective way of building a relationship with your audience - which really helps your site grow.

This chapter shows you how to set up and moderate comments as well as easy steps you can take to protect your blog from comment spam, which can make your site look unprofessional and uninviting.

Enabling and disabling comments

By default, comments are enabled in WordPress. To change whether comments are active or not, go to

Settings > Discussion. The third option down says:

Allow people to post comments on new articles

Unchecking that option closes comments, checking it allows them.

You can also decide to enable or disable comments for individual posts by checking or unchecking the *Allow Comments* option under the *Discussion* panel on any *Edit Post* or *Add New Post* screen. If you can't see the *Discussion* panel, click *Screen Options* towards the top right of the page and make sure *Discussion* is selected.

You can also allow comments on pages by using the same panels.

Moderating comments

There are two ways to know when your blog has a new comment. First, you'll get an email if you have *E-mail me whenever anyone posts a comment* checked on the *Settings > Discussion* page.

Second, you'll see the number of new comments next to *Comments* in the left menu of WordPress admin.

Clicking *Comments* will take you to a page where you can approve, delete and reply to comments.

Run your mouse over each comment and you'll see an extra menu with admin options appear that looks like this:

Approve | Reply | Quick Edit | Edit | Spam | Trash

Here's what the options do.

Approve - publishes the comment on your site.

Reply - opens a box under the comment so you can reply. When you're done, clicking the *Approve and Reply* button will publish both the original comment and your reply.

Quick Edit and *Edit* - both allow you to edit the reader's comment but *Quick Edit* lets you edit the comment without leaving the page, while *Edit* opens the comment editor in a new page.

Spam - marks the comment as a spam / junk comment and deletes it.

Trash - deletes the comment but doesn't mark it as spam.

Dealing with spam comments

Unfortunately, your email inbox isn't the only place spammers try to invade.

Sooner or later, you'll probably start getting spam comments. These are usually computer-generated and posted automatically to thousands of blogs in the hope of getting a link published in the comment text. Because the links often lead to scam sites or worse, it's a good idea to be pro-active in blocking them.

Luckily, WordPress has some pretty useful spam protection features built-in. Making sure the following features are activated means you'll prevent a lot of spam instantly.

First, on the *Settings > Discussion* page, make sure these options are checked:

Comment author must fill out name and e-mail

and

An administrator must always approve the comment

The first option will help to reduce automated spam and the second makes sure that no comment appears on your site unless approved by you. **Never uncheck this option**. If you do, your site will look like a spammer's convention in no time.

You should also install at least one anti-spam plugin. These work in a similar way to the spam filter in your email inbox - the idea is to detect spam and move it to a special folder.

The most popular anti-spam plugin for WordPress comes pre-installed. It's called Akismet. If you go to *Plugins > Installed Plugins* you should see it listed. If it's not already active, click the *Activate* link underneath it and then go to *Plugins > Akismet Configuration*. On this page you'll need to enter something called an *API Key* to activate the service (think of it like a password). It's a simple process to get an API Key, just follow the steps shown.

There are some other anti-spam plugins you can install which we'll go over in the Plugins chapter. But for now, activating those two WordPress settings along with Akismet should most spam comments.

Take care when approving comments that seem to be genuine - often they're written by spammers in disguise, trying to trick you into approving them. It's easy to fall for them if you haven't seen them before. Here's an example that was submitted to my blog:

Hey there, I think your website might be having browser compatibility issues. When I look at your blog in Opera, it looks fine but when opening in Internet Explorer, it has some overlapping. I just wanted to give you a quick heads up! Other then that, awesome blog!

Looks pretty genuine - and you'd almost be tempted to approve it because it seems like they're helping you out - but in fact the url was a link to a scam site. If you don't know the commenter, it's a good idea to play it safe and check the link they've left before approving the comment.

You can also google the comment text - often you'll find thousands of results for the same comment, confirming that it's a spam comment and should be deleted.

Posts vs. Pages

WordPress can publish not just Posts but Pages. The two are similar but there are some important differences.

Posts are meant to be displayed in chronological order so that it's easy for readers to find your newest posts. They can also have all the standard blog attributes applied to them like categories and tags.

Pages, on the other hand, are intended for content that wouldn't make sense as a blog post - things like About or Contact pages, or privacy policies and terms of service.

Because they're designed for this type of timeless content, they're not part of the blog structure. They can't be added to categories or tags and they don't appear on the homepage when they're first published. Usually, you'll create a page and then link to it from your header or footer (we cover how to do that in the Customizing WordPress section).

The process of creating content for posts and pages is more or less the same. In fact, if you go *Pages > Add New* you'll see the *Add New Page* screen is almost identical to the *Add New Post* screen.

Text formatting and adding media is done in the same way as for a post. But there are some key differences between posts and pages.

Pages can have sub-pages

Most of the time, pages are for stand-alone content like a contact page, so the lack of categories isn't a problem. But sometimes it's useful to organize pages into groups.

Let's say you have an About page and want two other pages - Contact and Who We Are - as sub-pages. Instead of using categories you can group pages together in parent / child relationships.

To do this, first publish the main About page.
Then, when you create each of your sub-pages,

use the *Page Attributes* panel in the right column of the *Add New Page* screen to select About as the *Parent*.

Now if you view *Pages > All Pages* you'll see the About page has the subpages underneath it. The page grouping will also appear on the top menu bar of the default WordPress theme.

Pages can have custom templates

In the *Page Attributes* panel you'll see another feature pages have that posts don't - templates.

Some WordPress themes give you a choice of page templates so you can use different features or layout options for a particular page. The default Twenty Fourteen theme that comes with WordPress has three page template options - the default layout, a contributor page (for showing an author profile and list posts by that author) and a full-width page layout with no sidebar.

These extra options let you adapt the design to better suit the content. For example, if you have a page with a lot of images you might want to use a page layout that has an extra wide content area to maximize the number of images you can show on the page.

To set a Page template, select the one you want to use from the *Page Attributes* panel. If you don't see an option to choose a template it means your theme doesn't offer a choice of templates.

After selecting the new layout, click the *Update* button.

How do I choose whether to publish content as posts or pages?

Most sites use a combination of both pages and posts. Three common site structures are:

1. **Blog**
Posts for the content with a couple of Pages for non-blog content like About and Contact.

2. Business or organization website

For this type of site there's usually lots of evergreen information like details of products, services, staff, FAQs, etc.. These should be published as pages. You'll probably also want to publish blog posts to keep visitors up-to-date about your organization.

3. Online store

If you're running an ecommerce store or product catalog site, the best option is usually to use pages for your products, with listings grouped into product types by using the parent / child feature. For example, you could have a main *Men's Apparel* page with sub-pages for *Shoes*, *Hats*, *Scarves*, etc.

If I change my mind later, can I convert a page to a post (or the other way around)?

There's no automatic way of converting between the two types. But you can manually convert any page into a post (or vice-versa) by copying content between page or post edit screens.

Part 3
Changing the Design

Customizing the Default WordPress Theme

One of the reasons WordPress is such a popular way of publishing websites is that it's so easy to make changes without having to edit programming code or hire a web developer or designer.

Like anything new, there's a learning curve but by the end of this chapter you'll be able to change the most important elements of your site - and even give it a complete makeover for free.

The default theme that comes with WordPress - called Twenty Fourteen - has lots of options to help you easily customize the look of your site. You can change the text in the header, add a header image, change the background color and more.

That said, you don't have to make any changes if you don't want to. Many people are happy with the default design and prefer to use it without making any changes. It's up to you.

This chapter shows you how to customize the standard theme. If you're using another theme, you'll find the options - and how to use them - are similar.

What is a WordPress theme?

Simply put, it's a collection of design templates that WordPress wraps around your content. Because the content is separate from the design, changing the design doesn't edit or delete the content. You can make changes to a theme or even switch to a completely new one without losing any of your blog posts or pages.

The first step is to go to *Appearance > Themes.*

On this page you'll see all the themes that are installed and ready to use on your site. Only one theme can be activated at a time and you'll see that at the top left, marked as *Active.*

Clicking on the image of the Active theme shows more information about the theme, along with links that let you customize the design: *Customize, Widgets, Menus, Header* and *Background.*

Note: not all themes offer all these features, so you may not see all of those links.

Let's start by clicking the *Customize* link.

This will take you to a screen like the one below. On the left are the customization options. On the right you'll see a live preview of your site.

Because the preview updates in real-time as you edit, there's no need to click Save to view changes. Only use the save button (at the top of the left column) when you're finished and ready for visitors to see the changes you've made.

The Twenty Fourteen theme gives you options in the left settings panel of *Site Title & Tagline, Colors, Background Image, Navigation* and *Static Front Page*. Clicking on each displays the options for that element. Let's go through each option.

Site Title & Tagline
Use this to edit, or remove completely, the text in your site header with the site name and tagline. In the image above, "My Awesome Blog" is the blog title and "Just another WordPress site" is the tagline. A good tagline helps new visitors understand quickly what your site is about. To edit the text, click on *Site Title & Tagline* and make your changes.

Colors
Here you can change the color of the header text or the page background. Clicking the *Select Color* option for either opens up a color picker. When you click on a color you'll see the color change in the site

preview panel on the right. Made a mistake? Clicking the *Default* button resets the color.

Background Image
Use this option if you'd rather use an image as your site background instead of a color.

Clicking the dropdown box shows an option to upload an image. As with the Media Library, you can either select a file from your computer, or drag and drop an image into the box. After uploading, you'll see a small version of the image appear - clicking on it brings up options to let you choose how the image will be displayed.

There are three settings.

Background Repeat
Whether the image will be repeated horizontally, vertically, in both directions (tiled) or not at all.

Background Position
Whether the image will be horizontally justified to the left, center or right.

Background Attachment
How the image behaves as the page is scrolled. *Fixed* keeps the image in the same position all the time, *Scroll* makes it move with the page content.

Navigation
This option sets which custom navigation menu to use for the main site menu. We'll cover how to create a custom menu in a later chapter.

Static Front Page
Lets you choose the type of content your homepage shows. The default is to show your latest blog posts, so if your site is primarily a blog you probably won't want to change that.

For other types of sites - where a "blog look" might not be what you want - you can choose to show one of your pages as your front page.

To do that, change the selector to *Static Page*. When you do that, you'll see two further options underneath: *Front page* and *Posts page*.

Front page is the page that will become your homepage, instead of your latest posts. In the image above, that will be a page called "Welcome".

The *Posts page* is the page that will show your latest blog posts instead of the homepage. In the image above, the posts will show on a page called "Blog".

Tip: You need to create this page first by going to *Pages > Add New*. Because WordPress automatically replaces the content of the *Post page* with a list of your latest posts, there's no need to add content to this page when you create it. Just give it a title and click *Publish*.

Saving or canceling changes

If you're happy with the changes you've made and want them to appear on your site, click *Save and Publish* at the top right of the settings panel.

To leave the Customize page without saving, click *Close* at the top. This will take you back to the main Themes page.

In this chapter, you've learned how easy it is to give your site your own design touch. But we've only skimmed the surface of what's possible. In the following chapters you'll discover more ways to customize your site so it stands out from the crowd.

Using Custom Header Images

Having a striking header image at the top of your site is a great way to stand out and make an immediate connection with visitors.

The page at *Appearance > Header* is where you'll find the tools to add images to your header. There are two steps involved.

First, selecting an image to use, then (if needed) resizing it to fit the header area using the Crop tool.

Selecting an image

There are two ways to set the image:

1. Use a new image by clicking the *Choose File* button to find an image on your computer and then clicking the *Upload* button. After uploading, you'll be taken to the *Crop Header Image* screen.

2. Click *Choose Image* to open the Media Library, selecting the one you want and clicking the *Set as header* button at the bottom right of the screen. This will take you to the *Crop Header Image* screen.

Using the Crop Header Image tool

The crop tool allows you to change the size and shape of an image to better fit your site design. After you've selected an image, you'll see a screen similar to the one below.

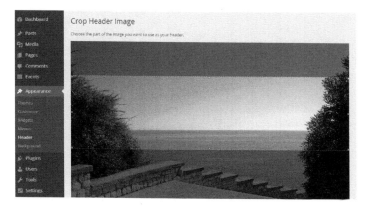

You can see the image has a lighter, rectangular area across the top. That's the area of the image that will become the header image - everything in the darker area will be cropped away.

Use your mouse to click and drag the crop area to the part of the image you want to use. You can also drag the edges of the crop area to resize it. When you're happy with the image crop, click the *Crop and Publish* button.

If you don't want to crop the image at all, click *Skip Cropping, Publish Image as is* at the bottom.

Now take a look at your website and you'll see the new header in place.

Showing different or random header images

Once you've added more than one header image, you'll see an extra option appear under *Uploaded Images* allowing you to choose which image to show on your header. There will also be an option to show random images.

Removing the header image

Click the button under the list of header images that says *Remove Header*. To start using a header image again, select the one you want to use and click *Save Changes*.

Adding Custom Navigation Menus

The default theme comes pre-configured to display links to your pages as the primary menu that runs across the top of the site.

ABOUT ▾   BLOG   EVENTS ▾   RECOMMENDED RESOU

In the example above, the site has pages called About, Blog and Recommended Resources - so Twenty Fourteen has added them automatically to the menu. If a new page is created, the theme will automatically add it to the menu and reorder the links alphabetically.

That works fine for many sites, so you might be happy to leave it as it is. But you can also customize the menu. You can create dropdown menus, links to blog categories and even links to other sites.

The first step is to head over to *Appearance > Menus*.

Type a name for your menu in the text box at the top of the create menu panel. The title won't appear on the site, so you just need a descriptive name for your own reference. Let's call it "Top Menu", as it'll be used across the top of the website. After you've added the title, click *Create Menu*.

At the top left of the page you'll see a tab called *Manage Locations*. Click the tab and Select *Top Menu* from the *Top primary menu* dropdown and click *Save*. This tells WordPress to use *Top Menu* as the primary menu across the site.

If you create additional menus later, the other menus will be listed as choices under *Top Primary Menu*.

Adding links to the menu

To learn how to add any type of element to a menu we're going to build one that has:

- A *Home* link on the left linking to the front page
- Links to *About* and *Contact* pages
- A list of blog categories
- An external link to another site

Adding the Home link and other pages to the menu

Click the *Edit Menus* tabs at the top. From the *Pages* panel on the left, select the checkbox of every page you want to appear on the custom menu.

If you have a lot of pages and can't find the ones you want, use the *View All* or the *Search* tab of the *Pages* panel to find them. You may need to use *View All* to see the option for *Home*.

Once all the pages for your menu are selected, click *Add to Menu*.

The new pages will appear in the main *Top Menu* panel. The order you see the pages listed is the order in which they'll appear on the top menu.

If you're happy with the order, click *Save Menu*. Otherwise, you can move the menu items by dragging and dropping them into the correct order before saving.

Removing a page from the menu

Click the arrow to the top right of the item to open the settings panel. Then click the *Remove* link to the bottom left.

Creating a dropdown select of pages

Sometimes, to create more space on the menu bar, you may want to create a dropdown select for two or more pages. Let's say we want to create a menu item that says About and shows links to two other pages -

Contact and Who We Are - when you run a mouse over the About link, like the image on the right.

To do that, first use the *Pages* panel to add the About, Contact and Who We Are pages to the menu. Then drag and drop Contact and Who We Are under and slightly to the right of About.

When you're done, it'll look like the image on the left.

When you've made all the changes you want to, don't forget to click *Save Menu* to make the new menu active on your site.

Adding category links

Adding Categories works in exactly the same way as adding Pages. Select the categories you want to show on the menu from the *Categories* panel on the left. If you want to use all the categories, click *Select All*. Then click *Add to Menu*.

You can reorder, remove categories or create dropdown selects in the same way as with pages.

Adding a link to another site

This is done with the *Custom Links* panel. Add the address of the link to the *URL* box and the text you want the link to say in the *Label* box. Then click *Add to Menu*.

Changing the wording of menu items

Sometimes you may want to use different wording on the menu from the actual page or category title - especially if the original title is too long to comfortably fit in the menu.

To edit the title that appears on the menu, click the arrow button to the top right of the menu item you want to shorten. Now edit the text inside *Navigation Label* and click the main *Save Menu* button at the end of the form.

Creating multiple custom menus

To make an additional menu, click the *create a new menu* link at of the *Edit Menus* panel. When you've created more than one custom menu, you can choose which menu is used on which part of your site by clicking the *Manage Locations* tab.

Removing a custom menu

Clicking the *Delete Menu* link near the bottom of the menu panel will remove it completely from WordPress. If you'd rather remove it from the site but keep all your settings so you can use again later, click the *Manage Locations* tab and change the dropdown menu to *select a menu* and click *Save Changes*.

Adding Dynamic Elements With Widgets

So far everything we've looked at in this section has been a way of changing your site design. Widgets, on the other hand, are a way of adding and customizing content and features. They allow you to add dynamic content to your site without needing to know web coding or programming.

The kind of things you can add with widgets include:

- Search boxes
- Newsletter subscription forms
- Automatically updating a list of recent posts
- Google AdSense / banner ad code

Head over to *Appearance > Widgets* to see a complete list of all widgets available for use with your WordPress theme.

The widgets you can use are in the *Available Widgets* column on the left. The panels in the column on the right are the areas of the theme that can have widgets added to them.

Available widgets vary from theme to theme, as do the areas where you can use them. In the case of Twenty Fourteen, there's a *Primary Sidebar, Content Sidebar* and *Footer Widget Area*.

To understand how the Widget page pictured above translates to what appears on our example site, let's take a closer look at the *Primary Sidebar* panel.

You can see there are a number of widgets already added to it, including Search, Recent Posts and Recent Comments. This configuration means the sidebar will have a search box at the top, an automatic list of recent posts underneath, followed by recent comments, and so on, down the list.

To add a widget to a sidebar, drag it with your mouse from the *Available Widgets* panel and drop it into the sidebar panel where you want the widget to display.

To remove a widget, do the opposite - drag it from the sidebar panel back to *Available Widgets*.

Creating a custom sidebar with widgets

Here's the step-by-step process to building a sidebar with widgets. We're going to create a sidebar with these items in this order:

1. A list of recent posts
2. Links to categories
3. A line or two of text about the site
4. Search box

To put this together we'll need these four widgets: Recent Posts, Categories, Text and Search.

By default, the *Primary Sidebar* has six widgets, only three of which we need. So the first step is to delete the Recent Comments, Archives and Meta widgets by dragging from the *Primary Sidebar* panel to *Available Widgets*.

Now we need to add the Text widget to use for a sentence or two about the website. Drag and drop the Text widget from *Available Widgets* into *Primary Sidebar*. The text widget should automatically pop open so you can add text to it.

If it doesn't, click the arrow to the right of the widget title bar to open the widget panel. Type a description of your site in the text box and click *Save*.

To change the order the widgets appear in, just drag and drop them round the Main Sidebar panel until you're happy.

When you're done, take a look at your site and you'll see your new sidebar.

Editing widget display options

Many widgets let you customize the title and other elements. To edit any widget, click the arrow to the right of the widget title. If you do that to the *Recent Posts* widget, for example, you'll see you can give it a different title and adjust the number of posts it shows.

Smart tip: If you want to remove a widget but keep the settings you've made, drag and drop it to the *Inactive Widgets* panel (under *Available Widgets*) instead of deleting it. When you want to reuse it, just drag it back to the sidebar panel - it'll reactivate with the saved settings.

How to add Google AdSense, banner ad code or Javascript widgets

You can add any kind of custom HTML, ad code or Javascript to your site by using the Text widget.

To add an AdSense unit, for example, drag a Text widget to the widget area where you want AdSense to display. Then copy the ad code from your AdSense account and paste it into the Text widget and click *Save*.

Smart tip: When adding advertising or programming code in a widget, make sure that *Automatically add paragraphs* at the bottom of the widget isn't checked, as that may break the code and cause it not to run correctly.

Finding Themes: Free vs. Premium

There are some great free themes out there, no question. The default theme that comes with WordPress is a good example. But premium themes have distinct advantages in at least 5 key areas:

1. **A more exclusive design**

Because fewer people buy premium themes than use free ones, premium themes make it easier to stand out from the crowd. That's even more true as premium themes tend to include many more customization options than freebies.

2. **Better support**

Theme developers know that happy customers mean more purchases and better word-of-mouth advertising. That's why you'll usually find the speed and quality of support is much better than with free themes.

3. **Quick, dependable upgrades**

As WordPress is upgraded, premium theme developers need to make sure their themes work with new WordPress features. That might not happen with a free theme, especially if it's just a part-time project for a hobby web developer.

4. **Peace-of-mind**

It's reassuring to know that because a premium theme is part of a company's business, it's always going to be kept up-to-date. The last thing you want is to be forced to look for another theme in a panic because your current one has stopped working correctly.

5. **Affiliate Programs**

Most themes can be displayed with a "Theme by..." an affiliate link to the theme store. Any time someone follows that link and buys a theme, you get a commission. Just a handful of commissions will repay the cost of the theme.

All in all, if you can afford to buy a premium theme (the general price range is $20 up to $95) it'll be a worthwhile investment.

There are a huge a number of companies selling good quality themes.

Here are some of the best, hand-picked for their range and quality of themes, the technical robustness of the theme, ease of customization, and customer support.

http://www.elegantthemes.com

http://www.inkthemes.com

http://www.ithemes.com

http://www.mojo-themes.com

http://www.organizedthemes.com

http://storefrontthemes.com

http://themify.me

http://themeforest.net

http://themefuse.com

http://www.theme-junkie.com

http://templatic.com

http://tokokoo.com

Finding free WordPress themes

Even if a premium theme isn't an option, you can still create a professional website with a free theme. But before you google "free wordpress themes" there's something important you should know.

Most free WordPress theme developers are honest - they love

WordPress, love design and are passionate about developing a quality theme. But there are some unscrupulous spammers out there who give away free themes in order to get thousands of links back to their sites. These links are often hidden in the footer of the theme and can't be removed without causing the theme to stop working.

Random searches on the internet are likely to lead you to websites distributing this kind of theme, even though they might look legitimate. Because of this, my advice is to stick to the trusted directories below to find free themes.

Each of these hand-picks and checks each theme to make sure the themes are spam-free.

http://wordpress.org/extend/themes/

As the home of WordPress, this is the first place you should look for a free theme. There are thousands to choose from and a sophisticated search engine means you can search by layout options (one, two or three-columns, for example) as well as by color scheme, customization options and design style.

You can either search the web directory at the link above, or search directly within WordPress by going to *Appearance > Themes* and selecting the *Install Themes* tab at the top. That has the bonus of allowing you to try themes out using the Live Preview feature before installing them. We'll look at how to do this is more detail in the next chapter.

Other reliable directories of free themes include:

http://www.dessign.net

http://www.fabthemes.com

http://www.s5themes.com

http://wpshower.com

Installing and Customizing Themes

As we've seen, the default WordPress theme can be easily customized and is pretty versatile. But what if you want a completely different look? Or a need a theme that's been developed for a specialist type of site like a photoblog, an online community or a magazine-style website?

The answer is to use a new WordPress theme.

The *Appearance > Themes* page is where you can see themes you already have and install new ones.

Previewing installed themes

Themes already installed are listed under *Available Themes*. When you click a theme screenshot, you'll see options for *Activate, Live Preview* and *Delete*.

Here's what they do.

Activate
This immediately makes the theme live on your site.

Live Preview
Opens up a preview of your site content with the theme. On the left of the preview page are settings you can use to customize the design before making it live. The options you can change vary from theme to theme but the chapter, "Customizing the Default WordPress Theme" at the start of this section covers how to customize the standard options.

Delete
Use this to completely remove a theme from your WordPress installation.

How to install a new theme

There are two easy ways to install a WordPress theme - searching the official WordPress themes directory or installing from a .zip file.

Installing a free theme from the official WordPress directory

Go to *Appearance > Themes* and click *Add New* at the top of the page.

This will take you to a form where you can search for themes by layout, color scheme, features and other attributes. If you already know the theme you want, you can search for it by name.

The search results will show you screenshots of each matching theme. You can click the *Preview* link under each to give it a test run. This will open a preview window showing a live version of the theme with test content.

If you decide not to keep the theme, click the *Close* link at the far left of the screen to go back to your search results.

To use a theme, click the *Install* button in the left column. This will download a copy of the theme to your WordPress admin area but it won't become live on your site until you click the *Activate* link.

Installing a theme from a zip file

If you've downloaded a theme from a directory or have bought a premium theme, the theme will be in a .zip file. To install, go to *Appearance > Themes* and click *Add New* at the top of the page.

Near the top you'll see a link that says *Upload*. Click that.

On the next page, use the *Choose File* button to find the .zip file on your computer. Then click the *Install Now* button. This will upload the .zip file to WordPress, unzip it and install it under *Available Themes*.

From there you can click *Live Preview* to edit the theme options before making it live, or *Activate* to start using the theme straight away.

Part 4
Extending WordPress with Plugins

Installing and Managing Plugins

We've already seen how easy it is to change the look and feel of WordPress by using custom themes and widgets. But WordPress has another powerful way of letting you customize your site - Plugins.

Put simply, a plugin is an add-on that adds extra functionality to WordPress, either in admin or to the public area of your site. It could be a completely new feature or an enhancement to one that already exists.

Examples of popular plugins include:

Akismet
One of the most popular anti-spam plugins for WordPress.

Contact Form 7
For adding an easy-to-customize contact form to your site.

WooCommerce
Turns any WordPress site into an online store.

BuddyPress
A plugin to create your own online community / social network.

As with themes, some plugins are free and some are premium.

Generally speaking, the quality of free plugins is extremely high - meaning it's normally possible to add the features you need to your site without needing to reach for your credit card.

One of the plugins I recommend is *ShareThis*, which automatically adds social sharing buttons to blog posts. To walk you through how to install a plugin, let's install *ShareThis* now.

The first step is to go to *Plugins > Add New*. On this page you have the choice of searching for plugins by keyword or browsing the plugin directory by tags.

Since we know the name of the plugin want to install, just type "ShareThis" in the search box near the top of the page and click the *Search Plugins* button.

On the search results page every plugin has a *Details* link. Clicking that will show more information about the plugin - often including screenshots of it in use. Because there are usually several plugins available for any particular search, this extra information can help you choose the right plugin. Anything that has the features you need and a four or five star rating is probably worth trying.

Back to our search results.

You should see *ShareThis* at the top of the results. Click the *Install Now* link.

Just in case you clicked it accidentally, WordPress will ask you to confirm that you really do want to install the plugin. Click OK to confirm.

After a moment you'll see a message like the one below, telling you the plugin is successfully installed.

Although the plugin is now installed, because it's not yet activated it's not doing anything. Click *Activate Plugin* to start the plugin.

At this point, some plugins may need additional settings edited before they begin working. Normally, you'll find them on the *Settings* menu under the name of your plugin. The *ShareThis* settings, for example, are under *Settings > ShareThis*.

Plugins with lots of settings often have their own section on the main admin menu.

ShareThis adds social buttons to your blog posts as soon as the plugin is activated, so you only need to go to the settings page if you want to change the style of buttons or which social networks are featured.

<u>Tip</u>: Whenever activating a plugin, always check your site to make sure there aren't error messages or other problems. If there are, deactivate the plugin and ask for help (see below).

How to deactivate and delete a plugin

The *Plugins > Installed Plugins* page shows a list of every plugin you have installed. Scroll down until you find the plugin you want to stop using, then click the *Deactivate* link under the plugin name.

After you see the "Plugin deactivated" message it's a good idea to take a look at your site to make sure switching off the plugin hasn't caused any errors.

If you're only temporarily deactivating a plugin and want to use it again later, you don't need to do anything else. When you want to re-activate the plugin, go back to the *Settings > Installed Plugins* page, find the plugin and click the *Activate* link.

If you know you definitely won't be using the plugin again, it's a good idea to delete the plugin entirely. To do that, click the *Delete* link that appears under the plugin name after it's been deactivated. WordPress will ask you to confirm that you really want to delete the plugin files. Click *Yes, Delete these files* to confirm.

Getting help with plugins

Plugin misbehaving? Can't figure out how to get the plugin to work as you want? There are two places you can get help.

The first is directly from the plugin author. Check the settings page of the plugin for an FAQ or a link to a support page. Alternatively, find the plugin on the *Plugins > Installed Plugins* page - there should be a link to the plugin homepage there. Another good place to find answers is the the official WordPress plugins support forum:

http://wordpress.org/plugins/

First search for the name of your plugin you need help with, then click the link to the plugin homepage and follow the *Support* link. This will take you to a dedicated support forum for the plugin. You may find there's already an answer for the problem you're having. If not, post a question of your own.

Remember that many plugins are a part-time project for the developer so you may not get a reply straight away.

Recommended WordPress Plugins

The links in this chapter lead to pages in the WordPress plugin directory where you can find out more about the plugin and view screenshots.

Once you've decided to try a plugin, the easiest way to install it is to go back to WordPress admin and search for it by name under *Plugins > Add New* and then install directly from the search results page. All plugins in the wordpress.org directory are free.

Akismet
http://wordpress.org/plugins/akismet/
One of the most popular plugins for fighting comment spam. This plugin comes with WordPress, so it should already be installed.

bbPress
http://wordpress.org/plugins/bbpress/
A sister project of WordPress, bbPress is an easy way to add a forum to your website.

BuddyPress
http://wordpress.org/plugins/buddypress/
Describing itself as "social networking in a box", BuddyPress is another sister project of WordPress that simplifies creating and running online communities and niche social networks.

Contact Form 7
http://wordpress.org/plugins/contact-form-7/
Lets you create contact forms that can be used anywhere on your site. In the next chapter there's a step-by-step guide to creating a contact form with this plugin.

Jetpack
http://wordpress.org/plugins/jetpack/
More than just a single plugin, Jetpack is an ever expanding suite of plugins that aims to make building a site easier. Everything from social network integration (including automatic cross-posting to Twitter, Facebook, Tumblr, Path, and LinkedIn), to featured content and writing plugins.

Google Analytics for WordPress

http://wordpress.org/plugins/google-analytics-for-wordpress/
Simple plugin to add a Google Analytics tracking code to your site for accurate visitor statistics.

Don't have a Google Analytics account? You can sign up for free here at http://www.google.com/analytics

Google AdSense Plugin

http://wordpress.org/plugins/adsense-plugin/
Provides an easy way to add the code needed to display AdSense, without needing to edit theme files.

Google XML Sitemaps

http://wordpress.org/plugins/google-sitemap-generator/
A plugin to generate a special file called an XML Sitemap which helps search engines index your content more easily. It automatically updates and lets Google, Yahoo and Bing know when you've added new content.

Growmap Anti Spambot Plugin

http://wordpress.org/plugins/growmap-anti-spambot-plugin/
Simple plugin that asks users to select a checkbox to confirm they're human. Because a spam robot can't check the box, automated spam comments are blocked. This is a much better solution than plugins that require visitors to type complicated and difficult to read words.

NextGEN Gallery

http://wordpress.org/plugins/nextgen-gallery/
WordPress has a simple image gallery option built-in, but if you need something more sophisticated try this plugin which has advanced features for building and displaying galleries.

ShareThis

http://wordpress.org/plugins/share-this
There are many plugins available to add social sharing buttons but this is one of the easiest to use. It also has in-depth user statistics available so you can see on which social networks your content is shared most.

TablePress

http://wordpress.org/plugins/tablepress/

If you're used to creating fancy looking tables in Word you might be disappointed to find there's no native support for tables in the post editor of WordPress. This plugin lets you create and reuse tables throughout your site.

Yet Another Related Posts Plugin

http://wordpress.org/plugins/yet-another-related-posts-plugin/
Automatically creates a list under each blog post of related posts your readers might be interested in, which helps keep readers on your site for longer.

WordPress Popular Posts

http://wordpress.org/plugins/wordpress-popular-posts/
Allows you to show lists of the most popular posts on your blog in a variety of layouts.

WP-DBManager

http://wordpress.org/plugins/wp-dbmanager/
Schedule automatic backups of your WordPress database.

WooCommerce

http://wordpress.org/extend/plugins/wp-e-commerce/
Turns your site into a fully-fledged online store.

WP No Category Base

http://wordpress.org/plugins/wp-no-category-base/
By default, WordPress adds the word "category" to category URLs. This plugin removes it, so that
http://www.yoursite.com/category/category-name/ becomes just *http://www.yoursite.com/category-name/* which is better for search engine optimization.

Adding a Contact Form with a Plugin

Having a contact page is pretty much a necessity for any website. Not only does it make you look more professional, it gives your visitors an easy way to send you fan mail :-)

The simplest way to add a contact form to WordPress is to use a plugin, and the simplest plugin I've found is called *Contact Form 7*.

One of the reasons I recommend this plugin is that it automatically creates a contact form when first installed that's perfect for most websites. You probably won't need to customize it. Below you can see what the default form looks like.

To install the plugin, head over to *Plugins > Add New*.

CONTACT

Your Name (required)

Your Email (required)

Subject

Your Message

SEND

Type "Contact Form 7" in the search box and click *Search Plugins*. On the search results page click *Install Now* under *Contact Form 7* and then click the *Activate Now* link on the page that follows.

Now take a look at the main admin menu on the left of the screen - you'll see a new option called *Contact*.

Clicking that heading takes you to a page that lists all the contact forms created with the plugin. The first time you see this page, you'll find there's just the default contact form listed. The page will look something like this:

Contact Forms Add New

Bulk Actions Apply

Title   Shortcode

Contact form 1   [contact-form-7 id="509" title="Contact form 1"]

Title   Shortcode

For each form you create, the plugin will generate a new *Shortcode*, which you can see listed in the right hand column. You can see that for my *Contact form 1* the shortcode is:

[contact-form-7 id="509" title="Contact form 1"].

Shortcodes are a kind of WordPress shorthand for a chunk of programming code. When you create a page or post that contains a shortcode, WordPress translates it into working programming code when the page is viewed in a browser. Although they might look a little scary when you first see them, they're much easier to use than real programming code.

To create a contact page for your site, first copy the shortcode from the *Contact* page in WordPress. If you want to add a form to an existing page open it via *Pages > All Pages*. Otherwise, create a new page by going *Pages > Add New*.

Then paste the shortcode into the main text box where you want the form to appear. It should look something like the image on the left. Once you've updated or published the page, make sure you test the form to be sure it's working properly.

How to customize the form

You can add or remove fields, edit the format of the email you receive and make other changes by clicking on the title of the form you want to edit on the *Contact* page in WordPress admin. It's a powerful plugin and there are so many options that covering them all is beyond the scope of this book. Instead, take a look at the excellent tutorials and FAQ provided by the plugin developer.

User Guide:
http://contactform7.com/docs/

FAQ / Troubleshooting:
http://contactform7.com/faq/

Part 5
How To Keep WordPress Secure

Making Automated Backups

Because WordPress is an open source project, there are hundreds of web developers contributing to and checking the programming code that WordPress runs on.

Add to that the millions of users around the world who use it every day, and you've got a robust and thoroughly tested web publishing platform.

That said, it's still important to take a few basic security precautions to protect your website and all the hard work you've put in to it.

In this section, we go through a few easy ways to keep your copy of WordPress - and your content - secure.

How would you feel if you lost your website overnight?

Unfortunately, server and database crashes, site hacking, virus and other security problems, while rare, do happen from time to time. If you don't make regular backups you risk losing all your hard work.

Luckily, it's easy to set up an automated system for WordPress.

There are two methods of backing up WordPress automatically - you can use an online service that takes care of everything for you, or you can install and configure a plugin.

Using an online service

For the number of features and value for money, I recommend two services.

BackupBuddy (http://ithemes.com/purchase/backupbuddy/) is both the easiest to use and the cheaper of the two. It's a straightforward plugin that makes automatic backups at regular intervals which you can download to your desktop, have emailed to you or sent to an online storage service like Dropbox or Amazon S3.

WebsiteDefender (http://www.websitedefender.com/) goes a step further, providing an automated backup service as well as checking your website for viruses and hack attempts, broken links and server misconfiguration problems. It will also remind you of critical security upgrades for WordPress and plugins. There are free and premium accounts (with a 30-day trial).

Setting up backups with a plugin

There are a number of plugins for making backups but many of them lack features, aren't reliable or require a level of technical skill that's beyond the average user.

That said, there is one great little plugin called *BackUpWordPress*.

The first thing is to install the plugin by going to *Plugins > Add New* and searching for *BackUpWordPress*. Once you've found it, click the usual *Install Now* and *Activate Plugin* links.

After activation, you should see a message across the top of your screen confirming that daily and weekly backups are being run. If you want to change the frequency of the backups, or get backups emailed to you, edit the settings at *Tools > Backups*.

One difference between the two backup methods to be aware of is that restoring your site from a backup made with *BackUpWordPress* needs to be done manually, while BackupBuddy can restore and move sites using the WordPress control panel.

Keeping WordPress Updated

New versions of WordPress are released several times a year. Sometimes a newer version brings new features, sometimes bug fixes and security improvements, sometimes both.

Whenever there's a version of WordPress available that's newer than the one you're using, you'll see a message like the one below across the top of WordPress admin.

When you see a message similar to that, <u>you should upgrade.</u>

Many people ignore the message, thinking it's not important or that upgrading is time-consuming or complicated. But using out-of-date software is the one of the most common security holes used to hack websites, so it's crucial to upgrade when you see that message.

It's not complicated or time-consuming. In fact, it only takes two steps.

First, click the link in the upgrade message that says *Please update now*.

On the next page you'll see a reminder that you should make a backup before upgrading. Upgrading rarely goes wrong, but if it does you'll be glad you have a backup so that you can rewind the changes. If you're not making regular backups see the previous chapter on making backups.

To start the upgrade process, click the button that says *Update Now*.

After a few moments, you'll see a message confirming that WordPress has been updated.

<u>Tip</u>: After an upgrade, it's always a good idea to check your site to make sure everything is still running ok.

Keeping Plugins updated

Just like WordPress itself, plugins are sometimes updated to provide new features, bug fixes and security improvements.

WordPress checks automatically for updates to
plugins. If any of your plugins need an update you'll
see a number next to *Updates* and *Plugins* on the left
menu.

Clicking *Updates* will take you to a page with a list of all the plugins that
should be updated.

Select the checkbox of the plugins you want to update, then click the
Update Plugins button. After a few seconds, you'll see a message that
your plugins have been updated.

Don't be confused if you still see a number next to the *Updates* header
on the left - that will disappear when you visit a new page in WordPress.

After a plugin upgrade, it's a good idea to visit a few pages on your site
to be sure the upgrade hasn't caused any problems. If you do see
something wrong, take a look at the chapter on Troubleshooting
WordPress.

FAQ and Troubleshooting

WordPress is the most reliable and robust publishing platform I've used, which is why I recommend it to friends and clients. Even so, there will be times when it misbehaves itself.

Here's a guide to the most likely problems you may encounter and how to fix them.

Lost password / login info

If you can't remember your password, click the Lost your password? link on the login screen. This will reset your password. For security reasons, WordPress can't just send you the old password. You have to generate a new one and have it emailed to you. If you aren't getting the email, remember to check your spam folders.

Database error messages

Most of the time, errors that mention not being able to connect to a database are problems with your hosting account, rather than WordPress. Nine times out of ten, these are fleeting connection issues and waiting for a few seconds before retrying is all you need to do.

If the error persists for more than a couple of minutes, or if you see it frequently, contact support at your hosting company, quoting the exact text of the error message.

Image uploading error messages

If you see error messages when you try to upload a particular image, try uploading a different one. If that works, there's probably something wrong with the first image.

Files with very long names, especially if they contain punctuation or other special characters, can sometimes cause problems. Give your file a short name that uses only letters and numbers and try uploading again.

If you can't upload any images at all, it may indicate a problem with file saving on your web server. These can be caused by upgrades to server software by your hosting company, or some other change that's crept in. If the error message mentions "permissions", that's almost certainly the problem.

In that case, the quickest solution is usually to contact your hosting company support team and explain that you think the WordPress uploads directory isn't saving uploads and quote the exact error message you see.

WordPress admin pages look weird

If the usual design of the admin area is gone and you're seeing large blank spaces with everything in the wrong place, it's likely that a file called a stylesheet hasn't loaded correctly. Try reloading the page, as that often fixes the problem.

If the problem appeared immediately after installing a plugin or theme and doesn't go away with a couple of page reloads, try deactivating the plugin or theme, to see if that restores the admin area.

Warning: Cannot modify header information – headers already sent by…

Most of the time, this error message appears after you install or upgrade a plugin or theme.

Sometimes it's a one-off problem, so visit another page to see if the message disappears. If it doesn't, and you've recently installed or upgraded a plugin, deactivate that plugin or theme to see if the message goes away.

If the problem only seems to be caused by one particular plugin or theme, contact the developer for help.

Where can I find the URL of my RSS feed?

An RSS feed is used by blog directories, feed readers and other apps to show links to your latest posts. WordPress creates an RSS feed automatically and you'll find it at:

http://www.yoursite.com/feed/

Remember to replace yoursite.com with your own domain.

There's a bar running across the top of my website that's not part of my design. How do I get rid of it?

In WordPress admin, click your profile icon at the top right of the page, then click *Edit My Profile*. Under *Personal Options*, uncheck *Show Toolbar when viewing site* and then click the *Update Profile* button at the bottom of the page.

How do I stop WordPress adding graphical emoticons?

By default, WordPress converts text like :-) and :-P to graphics. To stop that, go to *Settings > Writing* and uncheck the option at the top that says *Convert emoticons like :-) and :-P to graphics on display*. Then click *Save Changes* at the bottom of the page.

Why can't I delete the Uncategorized category?

If the delete option is missing from a category on the *Posts > Categories* page, it means that category is set as the default category and can't be removed. To delete the category, first go to *Settings > Writing* and change *Default Post Category* to a different category.

When you go back to *Posts > Categories*, you'll be able to delete the category as normal.

Fatal error: Call to undefined function...

This is another error that usually only appears immediately after activating a new plugin or theme, so the same advice applies - deactivate the plugin or theme to see if the error message goes away.

I **made a bunch of changes to my post / page and WordPress lost everything**

This can happen for a variety of reasons like the internet connection going down, or navigating away from the Edit screen without saving.

Luckily, WordPress has an autosave feature which can normally recover the lost text.

Go to either *Posts > All Posts* or *Pages > All Pages* to find the post or page that the text is missing from. Open up the post /page and look for a message at the top of the screen that says there's an autosave version available. Click the link in the message.

On the next page review the text to make sure it's what you want to restore. If it is, scroll right down to the bottom of the page and click the *Restore* link at the bottom right of the screen.

This will open up the normal editor with the restored text in it.

Important: You still need to click the *Save Draft* or *Update* button to save the changes.

Other places to get help

Because there are so many variations of problems you could face, it's impossible to provide a solution to every problem here.

One of the best places to get help for specific problem are the official WordPress support forums. Staffed by knowledgeable volunteers, you can normally get an answer quickly:

http://wordpress.org/support/

More WordPress Resources

One of the things I've always loved about WordPress is that there's a huge amount of information on every aspect of using and customizing the platform. With a little research you can find out how to achieve almost anything you want, either by using a plugin, widget or custom theme - or even by doing a little coding yourself.

Here are some of the best resources for taking your knowledge of WordPress further.

WordPress.org
http://www.wordpress.org
When it comes to WordPress, this is the Center of the Known Universe.

Specific sections of the site include:

WordPress Themes
http://wordpress.org/extend/themes/
Thousands of free themes by feature and design style.

WordPress Plugin Directory
http://wordpress.org/extend/plugins/
For almost any feature you can imagine, there's a plugin that can add it to your site. All the plugins in this directory are free.

WordPress Codex
http://codex.wordpress.org
If you want to learn how to create your own themes, plugins, widgets or templates, the official documentation should be your first point of reference.

WordPress Support
http://wordpress.org/support/
Stuck on a specific issue? The volunteers on the WordPress support forum can usually point you in the right direction.

LinkedIn WordPress Group
http://www.linkedin.com/groups?gid=154024&trk=hb_side_g

The official WordPress LinkedIn Group is a great place to ask questions, share ideas and make contacts.

Net Tuts+
http://net.tutsplus.com/tag/wordpress/
Comprehensive posts aimed at all levels, featuring code examples, inspiration and useful plugins.

Smashing Magazine
http://wp.smashingmagazine.com
Quite technical, so more of interest to developers or would-be developers.

We Love WP
http://www.welovewp.com
One of the most popular design galleries featuring thousands of examples of stand-out WP sites.

WPMU
http://wpmu.org
Packed full of articles to help you do more with WordPress. The site also covers BuddyPress, the sister project of WordPress which turns your website into a full social media network.

WP Beginner
http://www.wpbeginner.com
Plenty of tutorials aimed at the beginner and intermediate level, as well as practical articles on the wider aspects of running a website like getting traffic and search engine optimization.

WP Inspiration
http://wpinspiration.com
Gallery showcasing some of the best designed WordPress sites on the web.

Thank you for reading

If you've enjoyed reading this book, please consider writing a quick review on the Amazon page for the book. It really helps to spread the word so that more people can start making their own websites. Here's the link:

http://www.amazon.com/dp/B00AXBMH0W

Need more help? Something you'd like to ask? Feel free to email me at the address below.

Best,
Caimin Jones
hello@geniusstartup.com

Finally, here's the link to the video extras that go with this book:
http://www.geniusstartup.com/wordpress-step-by-step-extras/

Now you're up and running with WordPress you need visitors.

Keep reading for the bonus introductory guide to SEO for WordPress and details of my beginner's guide to SEO book.

BONUS CHAPTER
Search Engine Optimization Made Easy

Search Engine Optimization is the art of making sure your site is easily understood and indexed by search engines. Doing that makes it more likely your website or blog appears in search results for the keywords for which you want to be found.

WordPress does a good job of search engine optimization (SEO) out-of-the-box, but you can give yourself a boost by using the tips and tricks in this chapter.

Edit your permalink settings

If you haven't updated your permalink settings, WordPress creates site links in this format:

http://www.yoursite.com/?p=123

It's a good idea to change that because search engines rank URLs higher if they contain meaningful words.

Go to *Settings > Permalinks* and select Post name under Common Settings. Hit Save Changes and all your site links will be updated to use this format:

http://www.yoursite.com/your-post-title/

Keep your post slug short and meaningful

The post slug is the hyphenated group of words that form the last part of post and page URLs. In an address like *http://www.yoursite.com/your-post-title/* the post slug is the *your-post-title* part.

WordPress generates post slugs automatically as you write but you can edit them by clicking the Edit button just under the post title.

A good post slug relates to the post title but is only 2 - 4 words long. That means a good post slug for a title like *15 Great Australian Beers You've Never Heard Of* would be *great-australian-beers*. By removing short words like of, and, the and numbers; you're left with a punchy, keyword-rich post slug.

Keep your site loading fast

The loading time of your site is one of the factors that has a direct impact on your search engine rankings - faster sites rank higher. There are two things in particular which help:

1. Don't use too many plugins
Each one you use adds a little to the loading time, so use them sparingly. Deactivate and delete those you no longer need.

2. Don't clutter the sidebar too much
Again, the more things you add here, the longer your pages will take to load.

Use these recommended plugins

All in One SEO Pack
http://wordpress.org/extend/plugins/all-in-one-seo-pack/
Making more advanced SEO improvements is an in-depth task that not everyone has the time to do. This plugin is the easiest way to automatically fine-tune your website for search engines. It works great even without changing the default settings. There are other SEO plugins for WordPress but this is the easiest to use.

Google XML Sitemaps
http://wordpress.org/extend/plugins/google-sitemap-generator/
Generating a site map and automatically submitting it to search engines is the best way to get your new content indexed as quickly as possible. This plugin makes and updates sitemaps that can be read by Google, Yahoo and Bing.

Google Author Link
http://wordpress.org/extend/plugins/google-author-link/

A recent addition to Google search results is the inclusion of pictures of the author within search results. Because users are more likely to click results with images, it's really worth taking a few minutes to add this plugin.

Search Engine Optimization is an in-depth topic and something you need to master in order to have a successful website. But SEO can be confusing and, unfortunately, there are lots scammers and out-of-date info out there.

That's why I've written a companion book to *WordPress Websites Step-by-Step* called ***SEO Step-by-Step - The Complete Beginner's Guide to Getting Traffic from Google***. If you've enjoyed this book, you'll enjoy my SEO book.

Take a look at it here:
http://www.amazon.com/dp/B00AAY00ZQ

Made in the USA
San Bernardino, CA
25 September 2014